STUDY SMART: Learn and Apply Pocketbook

Drug-Drug Interactions

&

Lab Values

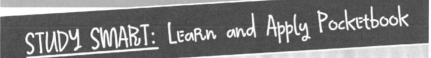

LAB VALUES:
CHOLESTEROL
BLOOD PRESSURE
DIABETES

DRUG DRUG INTERACTIONS:
WARFARIN
LITHIUM
MONOAMINE OXIDASE
GRAPEFRUIT

PHARMACY
TECHNICIANS

NURSES

PHARMACISTS

Pharmaduck

Thank You!

This guide is dedicated to anyone who wants to thrive and flourish their knowledge in the field of pharmacy. Whether you are scholar determined to earn a type of certificate, a doctorate degree, a grateful caregiver, or anyone at all, this pocket book will guide you through your classes in pharmacy school. Once again, thank you for your interest and investment in this guide, as this will set you forth to success, greatness, and step away from changing the world.

"And if you see me, smile and maybe give me a hug. That's important to me too."
- Jimmy V

"All that we see or seem is but a dream within a dream."
- Edgar Allen Poe

"Tell me, and I will forget. Show me, and I may remember. Involve me, and I will understand."
-Confucius

Dedicated to **Rex Thurgood** and all the students who are daring and dreaming to become great.

Terms of Use and Disclaimer

Let's Keep In Touch!

Reach out to us on social media. If you have any questions or concerns, please do not hesitate to reach us through the multiple social media platforms.

Facebook
Twitter
LinkedIn
Google+
About Me

Website:

Pharmaduck

Pharmaceuticals

Don't forget to join our mailing list!! We will send out free charts and continue to help develop brighter students that will care for the community, society, and the future of the world.

Mailing List:

Feedback:

Honest feedback and opinions are truly important in developing and building valuable material for students and future doctors. Please take your time and write us a review. The more reviews for our products, the faster we can produce updated versions free to the public.

Thank you again.

Free E-Book!

In addition to the pocketbooks to the public, we also have selected free e-books we would love to share with you in exchange for your interests in us!

These free e-books consists of drug charts, drug guidebooks, and leadership development guides.

Thank You!

Mission:

Ever felt that there are too many drugs to remember? Not only to remember, but to recall their generic names, brand names, indications, mechanism of actions, drug-drug interactions, and so… the list continues and continues and continues.

For me, when I was in pharmacy school, my professors tirelessly taught us complex concepts day after day after day, until we hit the "week", or better yet, the "night" before and cram all the scratches of notes, hour plus long podcast recordings, and dry powerpoint presentations for our midterm. Now, don't make me go into what happens during finals week and the aftermath of waiting to see your final grade after taking the final… we all we know how that feels…So let's not get into that.

Long story short, pharmacy school is a journey…some might call it a marathon (shout out to Prefontaine) and some might call it a quickie (shout out to Draymond). Nevertheless, these moments we spend in pharmacy school are the golden 20's or 30's or for some of us 40's…and these moments should be spent building covalent relationships with classmates, professors, and mentors.

After my years of doing what I love the most, I noticed that pharmacy students are capable of much more than they are taught in school. In this time of age, technology allows pharmacy students to look up medication information in a heartbeat. However, overtime students complain about feeling burnt out, anxious, depressed, and begin to bamboozle each other to compete for their life-long and successful career.

What has helped me, my mentees, friends and patients engrain pharmacy material effectively and efficiently is learning and understanding the concepts visually. Visual understanding and imagination presents great promises in achieving patient-centered care. The books, charts, and materials provided are here as a compass, to guide you to the right direction to strengthen your skills as a health care provider. Soar until you fly freely and understand visually.

-Pharmaduck

CHAPTER ONE

Blood Tests

What Are Blood Tests?

Blood tests help doctors check for certain diseases and conditions. They also help check the function of your organs and show how well treatments are working. Specifically, blood tests can help doctors:

- Evaluate how well organs—such as the kidneys, liver, thyroid, and heart—are working
- Diagnose diseases and conditions such as cancer, HIV/AIDS, diabetes, anemia (uh-NEE-me-eh), and coronary heart disease
- Find out whether you have risk factors for heart disease
- Check whether medicines you're taking are working
- Assess how well your blood is clotting

Overview

Blood tests are very common. When you have routine checkups, your doctor may recommend blood tests to see how your body is working.

Many blood tests don't require any special preparations. For some, you may need to fast (not eat any food) for 8 to 12 hours before the test. Your doctor will let you know how to prepare for blood tests.

During a blood test, a small sample of blood is taken from your body. It's usually drawn from a vein in your arm using a needle. A finger prick also might be used.

The procedure usually is quick and easy, although it may cause some short-term discomfort. Most people don't have serious reactions to having blood drawn.

Laboratory (lab) workers draw the blood and analyze it. They use either whole blood to count blood cells, or they separate the blood cells from the fluid that contains them. This fluid is called plasma or serum.

The fluid is used to measure different substances in the blood. The results can help detect health problems in early stages, when treatments or lifestyle changes may work best.

Doctors can't diagnose many diseases and medical problems with blood tests alone. Your doctor may consider other factors to confirm a diagnosis. These factors can include your signs and symptoms, your medical history, your vital signs (blood pressure, breathing, pulse, and temperature), and results from other tests and procedures.

Types of Blood Tests

Some of the most common blood tests are:
- A complete blood count (CBC)
- Blood chemistry tests
- Blood enzyme tests
- Blood tests to assess heart disease risk

Complete Blood Count

The CBC is one of the most common blood tests. It's often done as part of a routine checkup.

The CBC can help detect blood diseases and disorders, such as anemia, infections, clotting problems, blood cancers, and immune system disorders. This test measures many different parts of your blood, as discussed in the following paragraphs.

Red Blood Cells

Red blood cells carry oxygen from your lungs to the rest of your body. Abnormal red blood cell levels may be a sign of anemia, dehydration (too little fluid in the body), bleeding, or another disorder.

White Blood Cells

White blood cells are part of your immune system, which fights infections and diseases. Abnormal white blood cell levels may be a sign of infection, blood cancer, or an immune system disorder.

A CBC measures the overall number of white blood cells in your blood. A CBC with differential looks at the amounts of different types of white blood cells in your blood.

Platelets

Platelets (PLATE-lets) are blood cell fragments that help your blood clot. They stick together to seal cuts or breaks on blood vessel walls and stop bleeding.

Abnormal platelet levels may be a sign of a bleeding disorder (not enough clotting) or a thrombotic disorder (too much clotting).

Hemoglobin

Hemoglobin (HEE-muh-glow-bin) is an iron-rich protein in red blood cells that carries oxygen. Abnormal hemoglobin levels may be a sign of anemia, <u>sickle cell anemia</u>, <u>thalassemia</u> (thal-a-SE-me-ah), or other blood disorders.

If you have diabetes, excess glucose in your blood can attach to hemoglobin and raise the level of hemoglobin A1c.

Hematocrit

Hematocrit (hee-MAT-oh-crit) is a measure of how much space red blood cells take up in your blood. A high hematocrit level might mean you're dehydrated. A low hematocrit level might mean you have anemia. Abnormal hematocrit levels also may be a sign of a blood or bone marrow disorder.

Mean Corpuscular Volume

Mean corpuscular (kor-PUS-kyu-lar) volume (MCV) is a measure of the average size of your red blood cells. Abnormal MCV levels may be a sign of anemia or thalassemia.

Blood Chemistry Tests/Basic Metabolic Panel

The basic metabolic panel (BMP) is a group of tests that measures different chemicals in the blood. These tests usually are done on the fluid (plasma) part of blood. The tests can give doctors information about your muscles (including the heart), bones, and organs, such as the kidneys and liver.

The BMP includes blood glucose, calcium, and electrolyte tests, as well as blood tests that measure kidney function. Some of these tests require you to fast (not eat any food) before the test, and others don't. Your doctor will tell you how to prepare for the test(s) you're having.

Blood Glucose

Glucose is a type of sugar that the body uses for energy. Abnormal glucose levels in your blood may be a sign of diabetes.

For some blood glucose tests, you have to fast before your blood is drawn. Other blood glucose tests are done after a meal or at any time with no preparation.

Calcium

Calcium is an important mineral in the body. Abnormal calcium levels in the blood may be a sign of kidney problems, bone disease, thyroid disease, cancer, malnutrition, or another disorder.

Electrolytes

Electrolytes are minerals that help maintain fluid levels and acid-base balance in the body. They include sodium, potassium, bicarbonate, and chloride.

Abnormal electrolyte levels may be a sign of dehydration, kidney disease, liver disease, heart failure, high blood pressure, or other disorders.

Kidneys

Blood tests for kidney function measure levels of blood urea nitrogen (BUN) and creatinine (kre-AT-ih-neen). Both of these are waste products that the kidneys filter out of the body. Abnormal BUN and creatinine levels may be signs of a kidney disease or disorder.

Blood Enzyme Tests

Enzymes are chemicals that help control chemical reactions in your body. There are many blood enzyme tests. This section focuses on blood enzyme tests used to check for heart attack. These include troponin and creatine (KRE-ah-teen) kinase (CK) tests.

Troponin

Troponin is a muscle protein that helps your muscles contract. When muscle or heart cells are injured, troponin leaks out, and its levels in your blood rise.

For example, blood levels of troponin rise when you have a heart attack. For this reason, doctors often order troponin tests when patients have chest pain or other heart attack signs and symptoms.

Creatine Kinase

A blood product called CK-MB is released when the heart muscle is damaged. High levels of CK-MB in the blood can mean that you've had a heart attack.

Blood Tests To Assess Heart Disease Risk

A lipoprotein panel is a blood test that can help show whether you're at risk for coronary heart disease (CHD). This test looks at substances in your blood that carry cholesterol. A lipoprotein panel gives information about your:

- Total cholesterol.
- LDL ("bad") cholesterol. This is the main source of cholesterol buildup and blockages in the arteries. (For more information about blockages in the arteries,

go to the Diseases and Conditions Index Atherosclerosis article.)

- HDL ("good") cholesterol. This type of cholesterol helps decrease blockages in the arteries.
- Triglycerides. Triglycerides are a type of fat in your blood.

A lipoprotein panel measures the levels of LDL and HDL cholesterol and triglycerides in your blood. Abnormal cholesterol and triglyceride levels may be signs of increased risk for CHD.

Most people will need to fast for 9 to 12 hours before a lipoprotein panel.

Blood Clotting Tests

Blood clotting tests sometimes are called a coagulation (KO-ag-yu-LA-shun) panel. These tests check proteins in your blood that affect the blood clotting process.

Abnormal test results might suggest that you're at risk of bleeding or developing clots in your blood vessels.

Your doctor may recommend these tests if he or she thinks you have a disorder or disease related to blood clotting.

Blood clotting tests also are used to monitor people who are taking medicines to lower the risk of blood clots. Warfarin and heparin are two examples of such medicines.

CHAPTER TWO

What Do Lab Tests Show?

What Do Blood Tests Show?

Blood tests show whether the levels of different substances in your blood fall within a normal range.

For many blood substances, the normal range is the range of levels seen in 95 percent of healthy people in a certain group. For many tests, normal ranges vary depending on your age, gender, race, and other factors.

Your blood test results may fall outside the normal range for many reasons. Abnormal results might be a sign of a disorder or disease. Other factors—such as diet, menstrual cycle, physical activity level, alcohol intake, and medicines (both prescription and over the counter)—also can cause abnormal results.

Your doctor should discuss any unusual or abnormal blood test results with you. These results may or may not suggest a health problem.

Many diseases and medical problems can't be diagnosed with blood tests alone. However, blood tests can help you and your doctor learn more about your health. Blood tests also can help find potential problems early, when treatments or lifestyle changes may work best.

Result Ranges for Common Blood Tests

This section presents the result ranges for some of the most common blood tests.

NOTE: All values in this section are for adults only. They don't apply to children. Talk to your child's doctor about values on blood tests for children.

Complete Blood Count

The table below shows some normal ranges for different parts of the complete blood count (CBC) test. Some of the normal ranges differ between men and women. Other factors, such as age and race, also may affect normal ranges.

Your doctor should discuss your results with you. He or she will advise you further if your results are outside the normal range for your group.

Test	Normal Range Results*
Red blood cell (varies with altitude)	Male: 5 to 6 million cells/mcL Female: 4 to 5 million cells/mcL
White blood cell	4,500 to 10,000 cells/mcL
Platelets	140,000 to 450,000 cells/mcL
Hemoglobin (varies with altitude)	Male: 14 to 17 gm/dL Female: 12 to 15 gm/dL
Hematocrit (varies with altitude)	Male: 41% to 50% Female: 36% to 44%
Mean corpuscular volume	80 to 95 femtoliter†

* Cells/mcL = cells per microliter; gm/dL = grams per deciliter.

† A femtoliter is a measure of volume.

Blood Glucose

This table shows the ranges for blood glucose levels after 8 to 12 hours of fasting (not eating). It shows the normal range and the abnormal ranges that are a sign of prediabetes or diabetes.

Plasma Glucose Results (mg/dL)*	Diagnosis
70 to 99	Normal
100 to 125	Prediabetes
126 and above	Diabetes†

* mg/dL = milligrams per deciliter.

† The test is repeated on another day to confirm the results.

Lipoprotein Panel

The table below shows ranges for total cholesterol, LDL ("bad") cholesterol, and HDL ("good") cholesterol levels after 9 to 12 hours of fasting. High blood cholesterol is a risk factor for coronary heart disease.

Your doctor should discuss your results with you. He or she will advise you further if your results are outside the desirable range.

Total Cholesterol Level	Total Cholesterol Category
Less than 200 mg/dL	Desirable
200–239 mg/dL	Borderline high
240 mg/dL and above	High
LDL Cholesterol Level	**LDL Cholesterol Category**
Less than 100 mg/dL	Optimal
100–129 mg/dL	Near optimal/above optimal
130–159 mg/dL	Borderline high
160–189 mg/dL	High

190 mg/dL and above	Very high
HDL Cholesterol Level	**HDL Cholesterol Category**
Less than 40 mg/dL	A major risk factor for heart disease
40–59 mg/dL	The higher, the better
60 mg/dL and above	Considered protective against heart disease

Common CBC Lab Values

Complete blood count (CBC) Adults		
	Male	Female
Hemoglobin (g/dl)	13 – 18	12.0 - 15.0
Hematocrit (%)	38 – 50	35 – 44.5
RBC's (x 10^6 /ml)	4.3 - 5.7	4.0 – 5.03

Complete blood count (CBC)	
WBC	5-10 x 10^3/uL
Platelet count	150,000 to 450,000 x 10^3/uL
Albumin	3.2 – 5.5 g/dl
Alkaline phosphatase (Adults: 25-60)	40 - 145 IU/L
Ammonia	15 – 45 mcg/dl
Bilirubin, total	0.1 - 1.1 mg/dl
AST	10 – 40 units per liter
ALT	8- 58 units per liter
Electrolytes	
Calcium	8.5 - 10.3 mg/dL
Chloride	95 - 105 mEq/L
Magnesium	1.5 - 2.4 mEq/L
Phosphate	2.5 - 4.5 mg/dL
Potassium	3.5 - 5 mEq/L
Sodium	135 - 145 mEq/L

CHAPTER THREE

Cholesterol Levels

LDL Cholesterol - Primary Target of Therapy

<100	Optimal
100-129	Near Optimal/Above Optimal
130-159	Borderline High
160-189	High
≥190	Very high

Total Cholesterol

<200	Desirable
200-239	Borderline High
≥ 240	High

HDL Cholesterol

<40	Low
≥60	High

LDL Cholesterol Goals and Cutpoints for Therapeutic Lifestyle Changes (TLC) and Drug Therapy in Different Risk Categories.

Risk Category	LDL Goal	LDL Level at Which to Initiate Therapeutic Lifestyle Changes (TLC)	LDL Level at Which to Consider Drug Therapy
CHD or CHD Risk Equivalents (10-year risk >20%)	<100 mg/dL	≥100 mg/dL	≥130 mg/dL (100-129 mg/dL: drug optional)*
2+ Risk Factors (10-year risk ≤ 20%)	<130 mg/dL	≥130 mg/dL	10-year risk 10-20%: ≥130 mg/dL 10-year risk <10%: ≥160 mg/dL
0-1 Risk Factor**	<160 mg/dL	≥160 mg/dL	≥190 mg/dL (160-189 mg/dL: LDL-lowering drug optional)

Clinical Identification of the Metabolic Syndrome - Any 3 of the Following:

Risk Factor	Defining Level
Abdominal obesity* Men Women	Waist circumference** >102 cm (>40 in) >88 cm (>35 in)
Triglycerides	≥150 mg/dL
HDL cholesterol Men Women	<40 mg/dl <50 mg/dl
blood pressure	≥130/ ≥85 mmHg
Fasting glucose	≥110 mg/dL

Comparison of LDL Cholesterol and Non-HDL Cholesterol Goals for Three Risk Categories

Risk Category	LDL Goal (mg/dL)	Non-HDL Goal (mg/dL)
CHD and CHD Risk Equivalent (10-year risk for CHD >20%)	<100	<130
Multiple (2+) Risk Factors and 10-year risk $\leq$ 20%	<130	<160
0-1 Risk Factor	<160	<190

Let's Keep In Touch!

Reach out to us on social media. If you have any questions or concerns, please do not hesitate to reach us through the multiple social media platforms.

Facebook

Twitter

LinkedIn

Google+

About Me

Website:

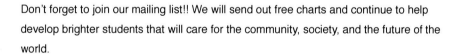

Don't forget to join our mailing list!! We will send out free charts and continue to help develop brighter students that will care for the community, society, and the future of the world.

Mailing List:

<u>Free E-Book:</u>

In addition to the pocketbooks to the public, we also have selected free e-books we would love to share with you in exchange for your interests in us!

These free e-books consists of drug charts, drug guidebooks, and leadership development guides.

Thank You!

Chapter Four

Importance of Blood Pressure

Measuring Blood Pressure

Blood pressure is the force of blood pushing against the walls of the arteries as the heart pumps blood. High blood pressure, sometimes called hypertension, happens when this force is too high. Health care workers check blood pressure readings the same way for children, teens, and adults. They use a gauge, stethoscope or electronic sensor, and a blood pressure cuff. With this equipment, they measure:

- **Systolic Pressure:** blood pressure when the heart beats while pumping blood
- **Diastolic Pressure:** blood pressure when the heart is at rest between beats

Abnormal Blood Pressure

Abnormal increases in blood pressure are defined as having blood pressures higher than 120/80 mmHg. The following table outlines and defines high blood pressure severity levels.

Stages of High Blood Pressure in Adults

Stages	Systolic (top number)		Diastolic (bottom number)
Prehypertension	120–139	OR	80–89
High blood pressure Stage 1	140–159	OR	90–99
High blood pressure Stage 2	160 or higher	OR	100 or higher

The ranges in the table are blood pressure guides for adults who do not have any short-term serious illnesses. **People with diabetes or chronic kidney disease should keep their blood pressure below 130/80 mmHg.**

Although blood pressure increases seen in prehypertension are less than those used to diagnose high blood pressure, prehypertension can progress to high blood pressure and should be taken seriously. Over time, consistently high blood pressure weakens and damages your blood vessels, which can lead to complications.

Types of High Blood Pressure

There are two main types of high blood pressure: primary and secondary high blood pressure.

Primary High Blood Pressure

Primary, or essential, high blood pressure is the most common type of high blood pressure. This type of high blood pressure tends to develop over years as a person ages.

Secondary High Blood Pressure

Secondary high blood pressure is caused by another medical condition or use of certain medicines. This type usually resolves after the cause is treated or removed.

CHAPTER FIVE

Diabetes and A1C

How is the A1C test used to diagnose type 2 diabetes and prediabetes?

The A1C test can be used to diagnose type 2 diabetes and prediabetes alone or in combination with other diabetes tests. When the A1C test is used for diagnosis, the blood sample must be sent to a laboratory that uses an NGSP-certified method for analysis to ensure the results are standardized.

Blood samples analyzed in a health care provider's office, known as point-of-care (POC) tests, are not standardized for diagnosing diabetes. The following table provides the percentages that indicate diagnoses of normal, diabetes, and prediabetes according to A1C levels.

* Any test for diagnosis of diabetes requires confirmation with a second measurement unless there are clear symptoms of diabetes.	
Diagnosis*	**A1C Level**
Normal	below 5.7 percent
Diabetes	6.5 percent or above
Prediabetes	5.7 to 6.4 percent

Having prediabetes is a risk factor for getting type 2 diabetes. People with prediabetes may be retested each year. Within the prediabetes A1C range of 5.7 to 6.4 percent, the higher the A1C, the greater the risk of diabetes. Those with prediabetes are likely to develop type 2 diabetes within 10 years, but they can take steps to prevent or delay diabetes.

What are target blood sugar levels for people with diabetes?

A target is something that you aim for or try to reach. Your health care team may also use the term goal.

People with diabetes have blood sugar targets that they try to reach at different times of the day. These targets are:

Right before your meal	80 to 130
Two hours after the start of the meal	Below 180

CHAPTER SIX

Drug Drug Interactions

Drug Interactions with Warfarin

Important information to know when you are taking: Warfarin (Coumadin) and Vitamin K

The food you eat can affect how your medicine works. It is important to learn about possible drug-nutrient interactions for any medicines you take. This handout provides you with information about the interaction between warfarin (Coumadin) and vitamin K.

Why was warfarin (Coumadin) prescribed for you?

Warfarin (Coumadin) is a medicine prescribed for people at increased risk of forming blood clots. Sometimes medical conditions can make blood clot too easily and quickly. This could cause serious health problems because clots can block the flow of blood to the heart or brain. Warfarin (Coumadin) can prevent harmful blood clots from forming.

How does warfarin work?

Blood clots are formed through a series of chemical reactions in your body. Vitamin K is essential for those reactions. Warfarin (Coumadin) works by decreasing the activity of vitamin K; lengthening the time it takes for a clot to form.

International Normalized Ratio (INR) and Prothrombin Time (PT) are laboratory test values obtained from measurements of the time it takes blood to clot. Individuals at risk for developing blood clots take warfarin (Coumadin) to lengthen the usual time it takes for a clot to form, resulting in a prolonged INR/PT. Doctors usually measure the INR/PT every month in patients taking warfarin (Coumadin) to make sure it stays in the desired range.

How do I keep my vitamin K intake consistent?

Keep your intake of foods rich in vitamin K about the same each day. For example, you may plan to eat only ½ cup of these foods per day. If you like these foods and eat them often, you can eat more, but be consistent.

Do not a make any major changes in your intake of foods rich in vitamin K. For example, if you typically have a spinach salad daily, do not stop eating it entirely.

What foods are rich in vitamin K*?

Food	Serving Size	Vitamin K (mcg
Kale, cooked	1/2 cup	531
Spinach, cooked	1/2 cup	444
Collards, cooked	1/2 cup	418
Swiss chard, raw	1 cup	299
Swiss chard, cooked	1/2 cup	287
Mustard greens, raw	1 cup	279
Turnip greens, cooked	1/2 cup	265
Parsley, raw	1/4 cup	246
Broccoli, cooked	1 cup	220
Brussels sprouts, cooked	1 cup	219
Mustard greens, cooked	1/2 cup	210
Collards, raw	1 cup	184
Spinach, raw	1 cup	145
Turnip greens, raw	1 cup	138
Endive, raw	1 cup	116
Broccoli, raw	1 cup	89
Cabbage, cooked	1/2 cup	82
Green leaf lettuce	1 cup	71
Prunes, stewed	1 cup	65
Romaine lettuce, raw	1 cup	57
Asparagus	4 spears	48
Avocado	1 cup (cube, slice, puree)	30-48
Tuna, canned in oil	3 ounces	37
Blue/black-berries, raw	1 cup	29
Peas, cooked	1/2 cup	21

What else should you know about warfarin (Coumadin)?

Alcoholic Beverages Alcohol can affect your warfarin (Coumadin) dose and should be avoided. Check with your doctor or pharmacist about this issue and any questions you may have.

Dietary supplements and herbal medications Many dietary supplements can alter the INR/PT such as: arnica, bilberry, butchers broom, cat's claw, dong quai, feverfew, forskolin, garlic, ginger, ginkgo, horse chestnut, insositol hexaphosphate, licorice, melilot (sweet clover), pau d'arco, red clover, St. John's wort, sweet woodruff, turmeric, willow bark, and wheat grass. Much is unknown about dietary supplements. The safest policy is for individuals on warfarin (Coumadin) to avoid all dietary supplements unless your physician approves. This includes any vitamin/mineral supplements that list vitamin K on the label. If they are taken regularly on a daily basis, they pose less of a problem than if taken off and on.

Vitamin E supplements Evidence suggests that vitamin E has blood-thinning effects. Vitamin E intakes above 1,000 International Units (IU) per day may increase the risk of excess bleeding. Research suggests that doses up to 800 IU may be safe for individuals on warfarin (Coumadin), but the evidence is not conclusive. It is best to ask your physician about taking Vitamin E supplements while taking warfarin (Coumadin).

Antibiotics Some antibiotics can either lower vitamin K levels in the body or interfere with the activity of warfarin (Coumadin). Check with your physician or pharmacist about whether you will need to adjust your vitamin K intake or warfarin (Coumadin) dose when you take antibiotics.

What should I remember about warfarin (Coumadin) and vitamin K?

1. Follow your prescription exactly, and keep your follow-up appointments for blood tests such as the INR/PT. Warfarin (Coumadin) is a very important drug for you.

2. Keep vitamin K intake constant from day to day because warfarin (Coumadin) interacts with vitamin K in your body.

3. Avoid herbal products and dietary supplements that may affect vitamin K and warfarin (Coumadin) unless approved by a qualified health care provider.

Drug Interactions with Grapefruit

- Amiodarone (Cordarone®, Pacerone®)
- Buspirone (Buspar®)
- Carbamazepine (Tegretol®)
- Cyclosporine (Gengraf®, Neoral®)
- Lovastatin (Mevacor®)
- Nifedipine (Procardia®, Aldalat®)
- Simvastatin (Zocor®)
- Sirolimus (Rapamune®)
- Tacrolimus (Prograf®)

Eating and drinking some citrus fruits and juices and other ingredients can interact with drugs, such as the ones listed above. Intravenous (IV) versions of these drugs do not interact with food.

When taking any of these drugs by mouth, avoid eating and drinking:

- Grapefruit juice
- Fresh, canned, or frozen grapefruit
- Tangelos and pomelos
- Products that contain grapefruit, bitter orange, or Seville orange

Check labels of juices, juice blends, fruit drinks, marinades, marmalades, and sodas for these ingredients.

What is a drug-nutrient interaction?

A drug-nutrient interaction can occur when the food you eat affects how your medicine works. The effect of the medicine may be changed, or there may be serious side effects.

The fruits and ingredients listed above contain chemical compounds that can affect how some medicines are absorbed from the gastrointestinal tract. The absorption of some drugs can be increased or decreased so that the amount of drug in your body is not right.

Do other citrus fruits cause the same problem?

Other citrus fruits, such as lemons, tangerines, and sweet oranges (Blood, Clementine, Mandarin, and Naval) do not cause a problem when taken with these drugs.

What will happen if I accidentally eat grapefruit or any other ingredient listed above?

It is unlikely that accidentally eating or drinking a small amount of these products one time will cause serious problems. These ingredients can affect drug absorption for several days, however. Consult your doctor or pharmacist if you think that you are experiencing side effects.

What if I have always taken my medication with grapefruit?

It is recommended that you stop eating grapefruit. Tell your pharmacist and doctor that you have made this change.

What is the possibility that grapefruit and/or these other ingredients affect other drugs that I take?

While studies are still ongoing, it has been found that these ingredients may change the absorption of several prescription and over-the-counter drugs. Check with your pharmacist about other medications and/or any supplements that you are taking. There may be a drug-nutrient interaction.

Drug Interactions with Lithium

Guidelines

These diet guidelines will help you keep your lithium blood level stable:

* Drink 8 to 10 glasses of water or other liquids every day.

Drinking plenty of fluids is important while you are taking lithium. Not drinking enough liquids may cause lithium levels to rise. You may need even more liquids during hot weather and during exercise when you sweat heavily. To avoid weight gain, select water and other noncaloric beverages.

* Keep your salt intake about the same.

Do not begin a low salt diet without first talking with your doctor or pharmacist. Do not suddenly increase the salt in your diet either. Less salt may cause your lithium level to rise. More salt may cause your lithium level to fall.

Try to keep your intake of these salty foods about the same from day to day: luncheon meats, ham, sausage; canned or processed meats and fish; packaged mixes; most frozen entrees and meals; soups and broths; processed cheeses like American; salted snack foods; soy sauce; smoked foods; olives, pickles; tomato juice; most fast foods; salt, salt containing seasonings and condiments like ketchup and meat sauces.

* Keep your caffeine intake about the same.

Keep amounts of coffee, tea, cola, and other soft drinks with caffeine about the same from day to day. Less caffeine can cause your lithium level to increase; more caffeine can cause your lithium level to decrease.

* Avoid alcoholic beverages.

Check with your doctor or pharmacist about this issue and any questions you have.

* Take lithium with food or milk.

This will reduce possible digestive side effects like nausea, vomiting, diarrhea, and abdominal pain.

Special Instructions

If you have any questions about these instructions, ask your pharmacist, dietitian, doctor, or nurse.

Drug Interactions with MOAI

Important information to know when you take any of the following drugs:

- Monoamine Oxidase Inhibitor (MAOI) Medications:

- Phenelzine (Nardil)

- Tranylcypromine (Parnate)

- Isocarboxazid (Marplan)

- Selegiline (Eldepryl) only in doses above 10 mg/day

There can be a dangerous interaction between your medicine and tyramine, a substance found in some foods and beverages. For this reason, you must follow these dietary instructions from the day you start taking an MAOI medicine until 3 to 4 weeks after you stop taking it.

Tyramine is found in foods that are fermented, aged, or spoiled. Normally, an enzyme (called monoamine oxidase) in your digestive tract keeps tyramine levels within a safe range. But when you take an MAOI this enzyme can no longer work on tyramine. When tyramine levels increase, they can cause potentially serious reactions such as severe hypertension (high blood pressure), headaches, heart problems, nausea, vomiting, visual disturbances, and confusion. For this reason, you will need to avoid eating foods containing significant amounts of tyramine.

Do not eat or drink any of the following:

- All aged and mature cheeses. The only cheeses that are okay to eat are: cottage cheese, cream cheese, ricotta, part skim mozzarella and processed cheeses like American, if eaten before the expiration or "best if used by" date. It is best to eat these cheeses soon after opening to make sure that products are eaten when freshest.

- All improperly stored meats, fish, and poultry. See details under Guidelines section.

- Air dried sausages such as pepperoni, summer "dry" sausage, salami, pastrami, and mortadella.

- Alcoholic beverages. In particular, unpasteurized beers, including beers from microbreweries or on tap, are known to contain tyramine.

- Sauerkraut

- Fermented soy products including soy sauce, teriyaki, soybean paste, fermented bean curd (fermented tofu), miso soup, tamari, natto, shoyu, and tempeh.

- The following foods are rarely eaten in the U.S., so you may not be familiar with them.

Avoid: Fava or broad bean pods, banana peel and yeast spread such as Marmite or Vegemite.

Guidelines

All foods that you eat must be very fresh, or properly frozen. Store all fresh packaged meat, fish, poultry, and dairy products in the refrigerator/freezer immediately. Eat allowed refrigerated meat products within 3 to 4 days. Eat allowed refrigerated cheeses before the expiration or "best if used by" date. Avoid foods if you are unsure of their storage conditions.

Remember to stay away from combination foods that contain foods to be avoided such as cheese crackers, sub sandwiches, stir fried dishes containing soy sauce, etc. Pizza, lasagna, and other cheese containing dishes may be eaten only if made with "allowed" cheeses and toppings.

There are many medicines and dietary supplements you must avoid. Tell your doctor, dentist, or pharmacist that you are taking an MAOI medication before taking any dietary supplements or medicines (either over the counter or prescription). There is a risk of interaction with MAOIs and many diet or weight reducing drugs; sinus, hay fever, or cold medicines; nose sprays or drops; asthma inhalants or

tablets; cough medicines; and herbal products such as St. John's wort and Ginseng.

CHAPTER SEVEN

Common Controlled Drugs

List of Common Controlled Substances

DRUG NAME (alphabetically)

Actiq®	Levorphanol
Adderall®	Librium®
Alfenta®	Lorax®
Alfentanil	Lorazepam
Alprazolam	Lorcet®
Alzapam®	Lortab®
Ambien®	Lunesta®
Anexsia®	Mepergan®
Anodynos-DHC®	Meperidine
Astramorph®	Metadate®
Ativan®	Methadone
Attenta®	Methamphetamine
Azdone®	Methylin®
Benzedrine	Methylphenidate
Beta-phenyl-isopropylamine	Methylphenidate
Buprenex®	Morphine
Buprenorphine	Morphine Sulfate®
Butorphanol	MS Contin®
Carisoprodol	MSIR®

Chlorazepate	Noctec®
Chlordiazepoxide	Norcet®
Choral Hydrate	Norco®
Clonazepam	Novosecobarb®
Cocaine	Opium
Cocaine® Topical Solution	Opium Tincture®
Codeine	Oralet®
Codoxyn®	Oramorph SR®
Co-Gesic®	Oxazepam
Concerta®	Oxycet®
Dalmane®	Oxycodone
Damason-P®	OxyContin®
Darvocet-N®	OxyFAST®
Darvon®	OxyIR®
Darvon-N®	Percocet®
Daytrana®	Percodan-Demi®
Demerol®	Propacet®
Desoxyephedrine	Propoxyphene
Dexedrine®	ProSom®
Dextroamphetamine	Resoxyn®
Dextrostat®	Restoril®
Diazepam	Ritalin®
Diazepam®	Ritalina®
Dilaudid®	Ritaline®
Dilaudid-HP®	RMS®
Dolacet®	Rohypnol®
Dolophine®	Roxanol®
Dover's Powder®	Roxanol-SR®
Duadyne DHC®	Roxicet®

Duocet®	Roxicodone®
Duragesic®	Roxilox®
Duramorph®	Roxiprin®
E-Lor®	Rubifen®
Empirin®with Codeine	Secobarbital
Endocet®	Seconal®
Epimorph®	Serax®
Equasym®	Soma®
Estazolam	Stadol®
Fentanyl	Statex®
Fentanyl®	Sublimaze®
Ferndex®	Temazepam
Fiorinal® with Codeine	Tranxene®
Flunitrazepam	Triazolam
Flurazepam	Tylenol® with Codeine
Focalin®	Tylox®
Genagesic®	Uniserts®
Halcion®	Valium®
Hydrocet®	Valrelease®
Hydrocodone	Vi cod in®
Hydromorphone	Vicoprofen®
Hydrostat IR®	Wygesic®
Hy-Phen®	Xanax®
Infumorph®	Zetran®
Klonopin®	
Levo-Dromoran®	

Let's Keep In Touch!

Reach out to us on social media. If you have any questions or concerns, please do not hesitate to reach us through the multiple social media platforms.

<u>Facebook</u>
<u>Twitter</u>
<u>LinkedIn</u>
<u>Google+</u>
<u>About Me</u>

<u>Website:</u>

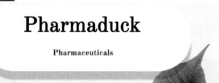

Don't forget to join our mailing list!! We will send out free charts and continue to help develop brighter students that will care for the community, society, and the future of the world.

<u>Mailing List:</u>

Free E-Book:

In addition to the pocketbooks to the public, we also have selected free e-books we would love to share with you in exchange for your interests in us!

These free e-books consists of drug charts, drug guidebooks, and leadership development guides.

Thank You!

Made in the USA
Coppell, TX
20 December 2019